mcr MCR

Meet Our New Student From

CHINA

Tamra Orr

Mitchell Lane PUBLISHERS

P.O. Box 196
Hockessin, Delaware 19707
Visit us on the web: www.mitchelllane.com
Comments? email us: mitchelllane@mitchelllane.com

Meet Our New Student From

Australia • **China** • Colombia • Great Britain • Haiti • Israel • Korea • Malaysia • Mexico • New Zealand • Nigeria • Tanzania

PUBLISHER'S NOTE: The facts on which the story in this book is based have been thoroughly researched. Documentation of such research can be found on page 44. While every possible effort has been made to ensure accuracy, the publisher will not assume liability for damages caused by inaccuracies in the data, and makes no warranty on the accuracy of the information contained herein.

To reflect current usage, we have chosen to use the secular era designations BCE ("before the common era") and CE ("of the common era") instead of the traditional designations BC ("before Christ") and AD (*anno Domini,* "in the year of the Lord").

Library of Congress Cataloging-in-Publication Data

Orr, Tamra.
  Meet our new student from China / by Tamra Orr.
       p. cm.
   Audience: 7-8.
   Includes bibliographical references and index.
   ISBN 978-1-58415-647-5 (library bound)
   1. China—Civilization—Juvenile literature. I. Title.
   DS721.O77 2009
   951—dc22
                                                    2008002275

Printing   1   2   3   4   5   6   7   8   9

                                                    PLB

CONTENTS

China

Shanghai is a busy city full of traffic, people, and skyscrapers. For the best view, you can ride to the top of the 88-story Jin Mao Tower (right) or take an even longer ride to the top of the 101-story Shanghai World Financial Center. When it opened in 2008, it was the third tallest building in the world.

A New Classroom

Chapter 1

Ashley walked into her classroom and came to a sudden stop. What happened? When she had left on Friday, it looked like it always did. Now, on Monday, it was completely different. There were new maps on the wall. There were two brightly colored paper lights hanging from the ceiling. There was a poster in the front with a large circle and a lot of animals around it. There was even a little package on each desk. Ashley hurried to her desk to take a closer look.

"What's going on?" asked Teresa, as she sat down in the desk next to Ashley's.

"I have no idea," replied Ashley. "What are these packages of long plastic sticks?"

"Those are chopsticks," said Tonio, as he sat down behind her. "I used them once when I went out to eat with a friend. They're like our forks and spoons."

Mrs. Vance clapped her hands. Everyone sat down and stopped talking.

FACTS ABOUT THE PEOPLE'S REPUBLIC OF CHINA

China Total Area
3,705,400 square miles
(9,596,000 square kilometers)

Population
1,330,044,600 (July 2008 estimate)

Capital City
Beijing

Religions
Daoism (Taoist), Buddhism; some Christianity
and Islam (Note: The government's official
religion is atheism.)

Languages
Standard Chinese or Mandarin
(Putonghua, based on the Beijing
dialect), Yue (Cantonese), Wu
(Shanghainese), Minbei (Fuzhou), Minnan
(Hokkien-Taiwanese), Xiang, Gan, Hakka
dialects, minority languages

Chief Exports
Machinery, electrical products, data
processing equipment, apparel, textiles,
steel, mobile phones, toys

Monetary Unit
Renminbi (or yuan)

"Good morning, everyone," she said. "How do you like the changes in our classroom?"

Sean raised his hand. "They look nice, Mrs. Vance, but what are they for?"

"We have a new student coming to Boulder City Elementary at the end of the week. Her name is Cui Ping," explained their teacher. The girl's name sounded like *kwee-ping.* "I wanted to make sure the classroom made her feel welcome. Now, based on what I have done in here, can anyone guess where Cui Ping might be from?"

"New York?" asked Kelly. Everyone laughed.

"No, somewhere outside the United States," suggested Mrs. Vance.

Ashley looked at the maps on the wall. She had an idea.

"Japan?" asked Rufus. Mrs. Vance shook her head.

"China?" asked Ashley.

"Very good, Ashley," said Mrs. Vance. "Cui Ping is from China's biggest city, Shanghai [shang-HYE]. Now, what ideas do you have for ways to welcome her to our class?"

The class had many ideas. Mrs. Vance wrote them down on the blackboard. When they had more than a dozen, the class stopped to vote on which ones they liked best. Making a snack was everyone's

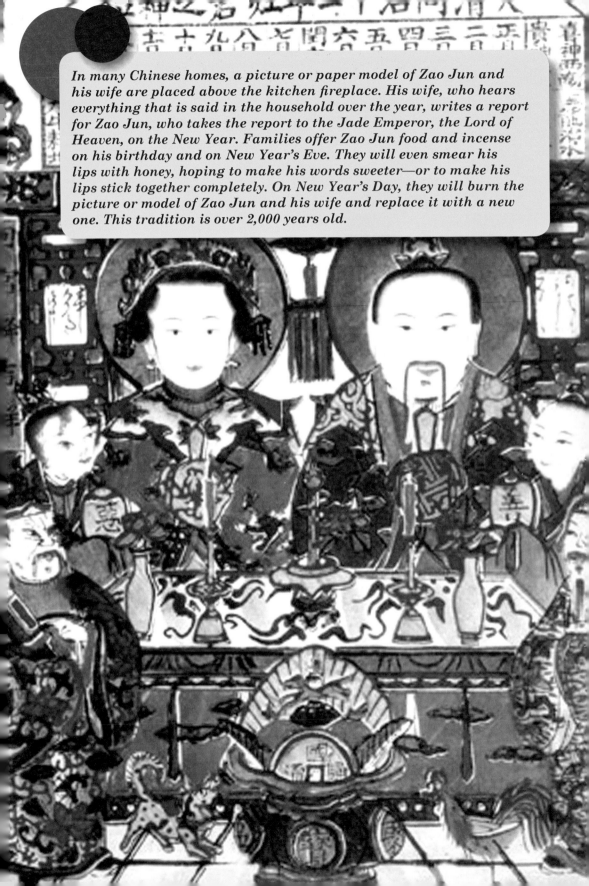

In many Chinese homes, a picture or paper model of Zao Jun and his wife are placed above the kitchen fireplace. His wife, who hears everything that is said in the household over the year, writes a report for Zao Jun, who takes the report to the Jade Emperor, the Lord of Heaven, on the New Year. Families offer Zao Jun food and incense on his birthday and on New Year's Eve. They will even smear his lips with honey, hoping to make his words sweeter—or to make his lips stick together completely. On New Year's Day, they will burn the picture or model of Zao Jun and his wife and replace it with a new one. This tradition is over 2,000 years old.

favorite idea. Next, they wanted to make some sort of craft.

"I like the paper lanterns you have by your desk," said Ashley. "Could we make more of those?"

"We sure can," replied Mrs. Vance. "In fact, that will be perfect. Cui Ping is coming here just about the time they celebrate the New Year in China. On the last day of their celebration, the children all make paper lanterns like this."

"But New Year's was weeks ago," objected Joshua.

"In the United States, it was," agreed the teacher. "But in China, they have a fifteen-day celebration that begins on the first day of a new moon. This means that it changes every year."

Ashley smiled. What a neat idea—a holiday that changed every year. She wondered what other fascinating things she would learn about China before the week was over.

A teacher and philosopher named Confucius lived in China from 551 to 479 BCE. He did a lot of studying and thinking. Then he shared what he had learned with others. He is known for many wise sayings, including: "If you enjoy what you do, you'll never work another day in your life." "What you do not want done to yourself, do not do to others." "I hear and I forget. I see and I remember. I do and I understand."

先師孔子行教像

楊清欽捐刻

A History Full of
Dynasties

Chapter

Experts have found evidence that people lived in China as long ago as 4,000 BCE. The two main groups were known as the Yangshao and the Lungshan. The Yangshao lived in the mountains of the north and west. Their homes were usually round and partly underground. They made beautiful pots, as well as tools such as axes and arrowheads. The Lungshan lived in the east. They also made pots, but their tools were made of bones and stones.

From about 1600 BCE to 1046 BCE, eastern China was controlled by the Shang **dynasty.** It was very large, with 30 kings and seven cities. In the center of each city was a palace for the emperor. Scattered around the palace were the mud and wood homes of the people who were artists of some kind. These artists made **bronze** weapons and vessels in which to carry things. Metal was hard to find then, so these items were highly prized. One of the most amazing

things these people did, however, was inventing writing. They were the first group in China to keep written records of their lives. They carved them on bones and turtle shells.

This bronze battle-ax is from the Shang Dynasty. It was used not only in combat, but also as a symbol of power and military strength. The tomb where it was found most likely belonged to a wealthy and powerful man.

In Xi'an, there are armies of soldiers that never move. They are the life-sized **terra-cotta** warriors that were built to guard a tomb more than 2,000 years ago. They were placed under the ground and were not found again until 1974. Imagine digging up an army of 8,099 guards still standing at attention!

Around 1040 BCE, the Zhou battled the Shang and won. The Zhou shared the land with the Shang but made them live in a separate area. They brought a new religion to the land, in which the sun and stars were worshiped. During the Zhou dynasty, laws were written down, marketplaces developed, and the population exploded.

	Dynasties		Time Period	Years in Power
三皇五帝	Three Sovereign Ones and the Five Emperors	sān huáng wǔ dì	before 2070 BCE	628+
夏	Xià	xià	2100 BCE–1600 BCE	470
商	Shang	shāng	1600 BCE–1046 BCE	554
西周	Western Zhou	xī zhōu	1046 BCE–771 BCE	275
東周	Eastern Zhou *Divided into*	dōng zhōu	770 BCE–256 BCE	514
春秋	Spring and Autumn Period	chūn qiū	722 BCE–476 BCE	246
戰國	Warring States Period	zhàn guó	475 BCE–221 BCE	254
秦	Qin	chín	221 BCE–206 BCE	15
西漢	Western Han	xī hàn	206 BCE–220 CE	414
新	Xin	xīn	9–26	15
東漢	Eastern Han	dōng hàn	25–220	195
三國	Three Kingdoms	sān guó	220–265	45
西晉	Western Jin	xī jìn	265–317	52
東晉	Eastern Jin	dōng jìn	317–420	103
南北朝	Southern and Northern	nán běi cháo	420–581	161
隋	Sui	suí	581–618	37
唐	Tang	táng	618–907	289
五代十國	Five Dynasties and Ten Kingdoms	wǔ dài shí guó	907–960	53
北宋	Northern Song	běi sòng	960–1127	167
南宋	Southern Song	nán sòng	1127–1279	152
遼	Liao	liáo	916–1125	209
金	Jin	jīn	1115–1234	119
元	Yuan	yuán	1271–1368	97
明	Ming	míng	1368–1644	276
清	Qing	chīng	1644–1912	267

Before 1912, there were a great many dynasties throughout China's history. The word *China* most likely comes from a powerful dynasty called the Qin (pronounced CHIN). They were in power from 221 to 206 BCE, and the people they ruled were often called the Ch'in.

The Great Wall of China was built over the course of centuries. It is the world's longest human-made structure. It is so large that some astronauts have claimed to be able to see it while orbiting the earth. It winds over 4,000 miles, crossing mountains and valleys, grasses and desert. It was originally built to protect the land from invaders, but today it symbolizes the pride of the Chinese people.

Over the next few centuries, more dynasties came and went. Each one brought new skills and ideas to China. One of the longest-ruling dynasties was the Song. They ruled for more than 200 years before they were defeated by Kublai Khan and the Mongols in 1279 CE. The Mongol dynasty, called Yuan, was a difficult one because the Mongols spoke a different language than the Chinese. They also wore different clothes and had different customs. These differences led to big problems. Eventually, the Mongols could no longer hold on to their rule. The Ming dynasty drove them out in 1368 and, in turn, was driven out by the Qing dynasty in 1644. The Qing ruled for 267 years—and then everything changed.

In 1911, frustrated by what was happening in their country, students and military officials worked to overthrow the Qing dynasty. In 1921, the **Communist Party of China** was formed. In 1949, Mao Zedong, the head of the Communist party, established the People's Republic of China. He had many plans for making China a better place to live. The plans raised new problems for the country. Between 1958 and 1961, thirty million Chinese died because there weren't enough jobs to earn money for food.

Mao Zedong (right) was the principal founder of the People's Republic of China and was responsible for the death of millions of people throughout the country. Here he speaks with Ho Chi Minh, the leader of the National Front for the Liberation of South Vietnam. The NLF's strategies and tactics were based on Mao's example.

When a huge earthquake and many aftershocks shook China in May 2008, people from all over the world scrambled to help the thousands of victims. Young Chinese students donated money for those families most in need. China held a three-day period of mourning for those people killed in the natural disaster.

In 1972, United States President Richard Nixon was allowed into China to visit. This was very unusual! People from other countries had not been allowed in China since 1949 when the communists took over. Nixon's visit opened a way for the two nations to communicate for the first time in history.

China has come a long way since 1949. In 2008, millions of people from all over the world would turn their eyes to China as Beijing hosted the Summer Olympic Games. There would be 302 events, played under the motto "One World, One Dream." To prepare for the games and all the visitors, China built or updated 36 gymnasiums and stadiums, plus 59 training centers.

China

The Oriental Pearl TV Tower soars up in the air in Shanghai. At 1,536 feet tall, it is the world's tallest TV and radio tower. The design of the tower rising up from the green grass makes it look like pearls shining on a plate of jade stone.

From a Forbidden City to
a Giant Toe

Chapter

3

One look at the map and you can tell that China is BIG! It is actually the fourth largest country in the world, right after Russia, Canada, and the United States. China spreads out over 3.7 million square miles. It has thousands of islands too, the biggest of which is Hainan.

China is surrounded by many other countries. To the north are Russia and Mongolia. On the west are Kazakhstan, Kyrgyzstan, Tajikistan, and Pakistan. On the south are India, Nepal, Bhutan, Myanmar (Burma), Laos, and Vietnam. To the east is the China Sea, which is part of the Pacific Ocean.

In a place this big, you can find weather of all kinds, from mild to extreme. In the south, it remains hot all year round, while in some of the river valleys, there are four distinct seasons. Northern winters can be extremely cold, with temperatures dropping far below zero. Summer temperatures can soar to over

China gets most of its rain during the summer monsoons, which bring strong winds, heavy rains, and high seas. Flooding is common, especially in the eastern provinces.

100 degrees Fahrenheit. The summer winds, or monsoons, can bring devastating storms.

With so many different kinds of weather, a variety of crops grow in China, including wheat, corn, barley, and sunflower seeds. The biggest crop of all is rice. It makes up almost half of the country's total crop output.

China is home to rare animals like the giant panda, the South China tiger, the finless porpoise,

The South China tiger, the finless porpoise, the Chinese alligator, and the giant panda are so rare that researchers are beginning to put their names on possible extinction lists.

and the Chinese alligator. Unusual trees and plants grow abundantly. The golden larch is a very rare tree whose coin-shaped leaves turn yellow in the fall. Herbal plants such as ginseng, Chinese wolfberry, and safflower are also common. The country's most treasured flower is the peony, which is known as the "king of flowers."

China has some amazing cities. The capital, Beijing, is more than 3,000 years old. Although it is full of history, it is very modern, with a population of almost 15 million people.

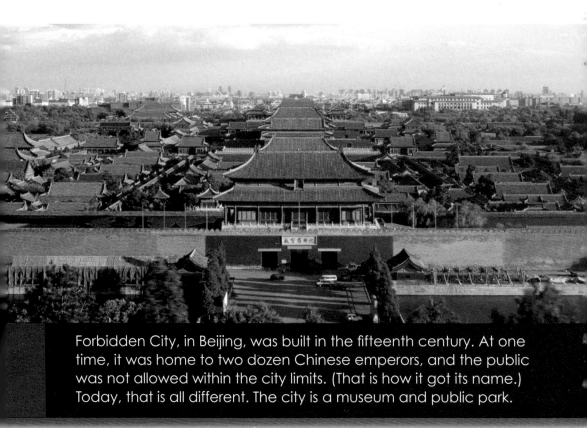

Forbidden City, in Beijing, was built in the fifteenth century. At one time, it was home to two dozen Chinese emperors, and the public was not allowed within the city limits. (That is how it got its name.) Today, that is all different. The city is a museum and public park.

The Giant Buddha of Leshan is the tallest stone Buddha statue in the world. Many people climb all the way down the steep stone stairs on the left to reach the monk's toes. The smallest toenail is wide enough for a person to sit on.

fun FACTS

China's Three Gorges Dam is the largest river dam in the world. It is five times the size of the Hoover Dam on the Nevada-Arizona border in the United States. At 7,660 feet long and 607 feet tall, it spans the Yangtze River in Yichang, Hubei. It contains enough steel to make 63 Eiffel Towers.

The biggest city in all of China is Shanghai. There are 18.6 million people living there. It is considered to be one of the busiest and most modern cities on the planet. It is hard to believe, when you see it today, that it was once just a small fishing village.

Another well-known city is Hong Kong. Its name means "fragrant harbor." It is an international place of business, where people from all over the world come to do business.

Some of the smaller cities in China have awesome treasures to visit. For example, in Chengdu is the Leshan Giant **Buddha**. A **monk** began carving it into the side of a mountain in 713 CE. It is about 233 feet tall, and just one of its toes is big enough to hold an entire dinner table!

In the city of Guilin, you can see limestone hills that reach up to 600 feet tall. They have fun names like Elephant Trunk Hill and Nine Horses Rock. These hills have been shaped by the wind and rain over 300 million years.

The Stone Forest (Shilin) of Kunming is considered to be the First Natural Wonder of the World. It stretches out over 96,000 acres, and the locals say, "If you have visited Kunming without seeing the Stone Forest, you have wasted your time." It features a wind cave and Dadieshui Waterfall with a 288-foot drop.

Rizhao City, or "City of Sunshine," is a coastal city of about three million people that uses the sun for nearly all its energy needs. Almost every home in this city is heated with **solar** water heaters. The traffic signals, streetlights, and park lights are also powered by solar cells. Homes use solar cooking, and 60,000 greenhouses in the area use solar panels to grow plants and flowers.

China

Rice fields, or paddies, must be covered with water for part of the growing season. Rice is the main crop in China, and rice farming provides jobs for many Chinese.

Life in
China

Chapter

China has the largest population of any country in the world! More than one *billion* people live there. The Chinese government was so worried about how many people lived in the country that in 1979, it passed a law called the One Child Policy. The law **dictates** that Chinese couples may have only one child. If you meet Chinese students, you will find that almost none of them has a brother or sister. If a family chooses to have another child, they may have to pay a fine or other penalties, so most families stop after one child.

More than 91 percent of the people in China are Han Chinese. The other 8 percent make up 55 different **ethnic** groups, including Zhuang, Hui, Tibetan, Manchu, Mongol, and Korean. The Han live all over the country, while the **minorities** (my-NAR-ih-tees) tend to live in the areas near the borders with other countries. The Yunnan Province is home to

There is an old saying about "all the tea in China"—meaning "a huge fortune." Like rice, tea is an important crop. Trained workers spend the day in the fields picking the best leaves.

more than 20 ethnic groups. All groups are treated equally. It is against the law to treat them differently.

Tibetans make up one of the ethnic groups in China. Tibet is part of China, found in the high plateau of the Himalaya mountains. Known as the "Roof of the World," it was once independent but was taken over by the Chinese in 1950. Half a century

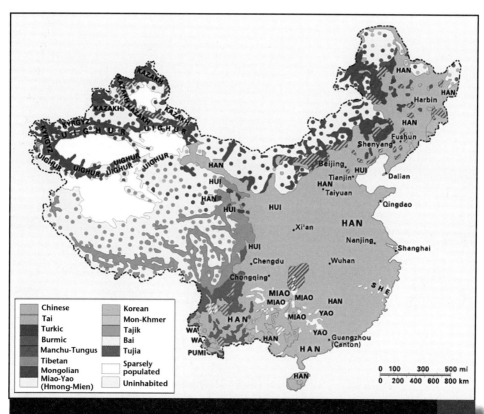

Ethnic groups tend to live near each other in China, with most of the Turkic in the northwest, the Tibetan in the central west, and the Mongolian in the central north.

The Potala Palace is Tibet's largest structure, covering more than 32 acres of land. Legend has it that it was built around a secret, sacred cave that was used by Emperor Songtsen Gampo in the seventh century. It has been expanded and repaired many times over the years. It has always served as the home for the Dalai Lama and his staff; however, the 14th Dalai Lama has lived in India, in exile, since 1959. Thousands of Tibetan pilgrims still come to visit and worship at the palace every day.

While many parts of China are quite modern, there are still people living in small villages. With their thatch-roofed homes, they live a simpler, slower life that has changed very little over the decades.

later, there is still great debate over whether or not Tibet should be considered its own country.

The Tibetan language is very challenging to learn. There are many different languages and **dialects** in China, and people from one region often struggle to understand the words of the people in the next.

Chapter 4

Learning how to speak Chinese is much harder than it may sound at first. There are at least six main language groups in this country, and more than 600 ways to speak them. To make it even more difficult, the tone of a Chinese word determines the meaning. It can be very confusing.

Mandarin is the official language—the one that is understood in the many cities, provinces, and villages throughout the country. Here are a few basic phrases in Mandarin:

ENGLISH	MANDARIN CHINESE
How are you?	Ni hao ma
Thank you	Xie xie
Goodbye, or See you again	Zai jian
Excuse me	Jie guo
Very good	Hen hao

School in China is very, very important. Parents spend more money on getting a good education for their children than anything other than food! The cost of private schools is high, but many families make great **sacrifices** to make sure their children get into them. Children are often reminded to work hard in school, and good grades are extremely important. Many Chinese children do not spend time playing with friends or doing other afterschool activities. Instead, they study and do their homework.

Showing off their solar-powered inventions are three students from the Hu Shan Road Elementary School in Qingdao. Their school is the first solar-powered school in China. Opened in March 2008, it provides heat to its 30 classrooms with a solar-powered heating system that turns on when the temperature falls below 65 degrees.

Most of them also spend their summers in school. Weekends are usually for lessons in other things, such as how to play a musical instrument, or for extra tutoring in the subjects that are the hardest to learn.

In China, many ethnic groups wear colorful headdresses as part of dressing up for holidays and special events. Some are made with beads, like the one Cui Ping wears, while others may be made with flowers, stones, gems, feathers or bones.

Huan Yin,
Cui Ping

Chapter

It had been an exciting week in Mrs. Vance's class. Everyone had learned a lot about China, and now they were all eager to meet someone who had lived there.

When Cui Ping walked through the door, Ashley was surprised to see that she was wearing jeans and a T-shirt, just like the other girls. She had hoped she would wear something Chinese, but then realized that Cui Ping was probably doing her best to fit in with the rest of the kids.

"Welcome to our class at Boulder City Elementary," said Mrs. Vance. "Let me show you your desk."

As Cui Ping walked, she looked up and saw the dozens of Chinese lanterns the students had made. She started to smile. When everyone was served a cup of hot tea and some almond cookies a few minutes later, her smile got even bigger.

"Did you see the signs we're wearing?" Ashley asked Cui Ping. "We found out what sign we were on the Chinese zodiac and drew a picture of the animal, then added our names. Most of us are either snakes or horses, like me."

The Chinese zodiac differs from the one most Americans are familiar with. Instead of being based on what month a person is born, this one is based on the year.

Cui Ping nodded. "I am a snake too," she said softly.

"What was your house like in Shanghai?" asked Sean. "Was it a pagoda?"

Cui Ping laughed. "No," she said. "It was just like one of your houses here."

Cui Ping's mother (left) and grandmother (middle) are happy to be in the United States. Already they have met their neighbors, Lin Xiang Yu (right) and her son.

"Do you have a lot of toys in China?" asked Kelly.

Cui Ping frowned. " I don't know what you mean," she said.

"That is an odd question, Kelly," agreed Mrs. Vance. "What did you mean?"

"Well," said Kelly slowly, "my brother and I were putting away our toys last night and I realized that most of them said they were made in China. I thought it must mean that China has more toys than other countries."

Cui Ping, Mrs. Vance, and the rest of the class laughed.

The *Emma Maersk* is the largest container vessel in the world. She is 1,300 feet long and is capable of carrying 156,907 metric tons (more than 4,000 containers). A crew of only thirteen people operates her. She makes regular stops in several ports in China, then delivers the goods around the world.

"You're right in a way," said Mrs. Vance. "China makes many products that are imported or brought into the United States. Many Chinese companies make clothes, computer games—and lots of toys—that Americans buy. Now, what other questions do you have for our new student, class?"

"What was your favorite game in China?" asked Joshua.

"It is Forcing the City Gates. Do you know that one?" No one in the class did.

"Can you show us how to play it?" asked Mrs. Vance.

Cui Ping stood up and said, "There are two teams. Each one has a captain. The teams stand in two lines, facing each other. They hold hands and sing,

He stuck a feather in his hat,
And hurried to the town
And children met him with a horse
For the gates were broken down.

"Then," Cui Ping continued, "one player runs at the other side and tries to break through."

"Hey, we know that one!" exclaimed Ashley. "We call that Red Rover."

"Whatever you call it," said Mrs. Vance, "it's fun—so let's head out to the playground and play a few rounds!"

Seesaw jumping is a popular game to play in China. Known as *tiaoban*, it uses a springboard almost 20 feet long and just over one foot wide. It is made out of a strong but bouncy wood. Sometimes the players do spins, backflips or somersaults while they are up in the air.

It was a full and fun day in Mrs. Vance's class. By the time the bell rang to go home, Cui Ping had had three almond cookies and four cups of tea, made two paper lanterns, played three rounds of Forcing the City Gates, and had more friends than she could have imagined.

Things You Will Need

An adult
2 large bowls
Measuring cups and spoons
Electric mixer
Wooden spoon
Waxed paper and table knife
Cookie sheet and spatula
Oven
Pot holder or oven mitt
Wire rack

Ingredients

1 cup shortening

¾ cup sugar

2 eggs

1 tablespoon almond extract

2¼ cups flour

½ teaspoon baking soda

¼ teaspoon salt

½ cup blanched almond halves

1 beaten egg

How To Make

Almond Cookies

Instructions

Have AN ADULT help you with this recipe, especially for all steps that use a hot oven.

1. In a large bowl with an electric mixer, cream the shortening and sugar.
2. Beat in the eggs, one at a time, and mix well.
3. Add the almond extract and mix.
4. In another bowl, sift together the flour, baking soda, and salt.
5. With a wooden spoon, gradually stir the flour mixture into the shortening. The dough should be fairly firm.
6. Divide the dough in half and roll each into a log about 1½ inches in diameter. Wrap in waxed paper and refrigerate for 4 hours.
7. Preheat the oven to 375°F.
8. Cut the dough crosswise into ¼-inch-thick slices. Place cookies on an ungreased cookie sheet.
9. Top each cookie with an almond half. Brush cookies lightly with beaten egg.
10. Bake for about 10 minutes, or until light golden brown. Cool on wire rack.

Make Your Own
Chinese Lantern

You Will Need

Stickers

Scissors

An adult to help you

Glue

Tape

Stapler

Construction paper

Glitter Glue

On the fifteenth day of the first **lunar** month in China is the Chinese Lantern Festival. Under a bright, full moon, thousands of colorful lanterns are hung outside. Each one has a puzzle on it that people read and try to figure out. As the night is lit by both moon and lanterns, the people celebrate by eating moon cakes and spending time with their families.

Instructions for Making a Chinese Lantern

Please do not use your lantern with candles! It is for decoration only.

1 Fold a rectangular piece of paper in half lengthwise. It should be a long, thin rectangle.

2 Make a series of cuts (a dozen or more) along the fold line. Do not cut all the way to the edge of the paper, however.

3 Unfold the paper. Glue or staple the short edges of the paper together.

4 From another piece of paper, cut a strip 6 inches long and ½ inch wide.

5 Glue or staple this strip of paper across one end of the lantern. This makes the handle.

6 Decorate your lantern with stickers or glitter and glue.

Further Reading

Books

Challen, Paul. *Life in Ancient China.* New York: Crabtree Publishing Company, 2004.

Cole, Joanna. *Ms. Frizzle's Adventures: Imperial China.* New York: Scholastic Press, 2005.

George, Charles, and Linda George. *Wonders of the World: The Clay Soldiers of China.* Bel Air, California: KidHaven Press, 2005.

Kah Joon, Liow. *A Musical Journey: From the Great Wall of China to the Water Towns of Jiangnan.* La Prairie, Québec, Canada: Silk Roads Networks, Inc., 2004.

Li, Yaw-Wen, et al. *Sweet and Sour: Tales from China.* Bel Air, California: Clarion Books, 2007.

Sebag-Montefiore, Hugh. *China (DK Eyewitness Books).* New York: DK Children's, 2007.

Works Consulted

Chai, May-lee, and Winberg Chai. *China A to Z: Everything You Need to Know to Understand Chinese Customs and Culture.* New York: Plume, 2007.

Cotterell, Arthur, and Laura Buller. *Ancient China.* New York: DK Publishing, 2005.

Fairbank, John King, and Merle Goldman. *China: A New History.* Cambridge, Massachusetts: Belknap Press, 2006.

Fry, Ying Ying. *Kids Like Me in China.* St. Paul, Minnesota: Yeong and Yeong Book Company, 2001.

Morton, W. Scott, and Charlton M. Lewis. *China: Its History and Culture.* Columbus, Ohio: McGraw-Hill Books, 2004.

On the Internet

Asian Info Organization: Chinese People
http://www.asianinfo.org/asianinfo/china/people.htm

Confucius Biography
http://www.crystalinks.com/confucius.html

Frankenstein, Paul. Condensed China.
http://condensedchina.com/

The Global Gourmet: China Almond Cookies
http://www.globalgourmet.com/destinations/china/almocook.html

International Rivers Organization: Three Gorges Dam
http://internationalrivers.org/en/china/three-gorges-dam

Minnesota State University: Timeline of Chinese Dynasties
http://www.mnsu.edu/emuseum/prehistory/china/timeline.html

Further Reading

Official Web Site of the Beijing 2008 Olympic Games
   http://en.beijing2008.cn/

EMBASSY
Embassy of the People's Republic of China in the United States
2300 Connecticut Ave., NW
Washington, DC 20008
Telephone: (202) 328-2500
Fax: (202) 588-0032
http://www.china-embassy.org/eng/

China's
Renminbi
(yuan)

Glossary

bronze—A brown metal made from a mixture of copper, tin, and usually some other elements.

Buddha (BOO-duh)—A representation of Gautama Buddha, a teacher who started the religion of Buddhism.

communist (KAH-myoo-nist)—A person who supports the ideas of communism, a system in which the community or government owns all property and businesses.

Dalai Lama (DAH-lee LAH-mah)—The political and spiritual leader of Tibet.

dialect (DYE-uh-lekt)—The way one group pronounces and uses a language that is different than how another group might speak the same language.

dictates (DIK-tayts)—Requires by law.

dynasty (DYE-nus-tee)—A line of rulers, usually from the same family.

ethnic (ETH-nik)—From a common culture, religion, language, or other bond.

exile (EK-zyl)—Absence from one's own country or home.

extinction (ek-STINK-shun)—Complete loss of life; gone forever.

lunar (LOO-nur)—Having to do with the moon.

minorities (my-NAR-ih-tees)—People in a part of a population that share a common background.

monk—A man who is a member of a religious order.

monsoon (mon-SOON)—A seasonal wind that brings in storms with heavy rains.

pagoda (puh-GOH-duh)—A temple or sacred building.

philosopher (fih-LAH-sih-fer)—A person who seeks wisdom.

province (PRAH-vintz)—A part of a country, similar to a state.

sacrifices (SAA-krih-fye-ses)—Giving up something important in order to get something else.

solar (SOH-lur)—Having to do with the sun or the sun's energy.

terra-cotta (tayr-uh-KAH-tuh)—A type of orange clay that has been fired in an oven.

Index

ABOUT THE AUTHOR

Tamra Orr is the author of more than 140 nonfiction books for children of all ages. She has a bachelor's degree in secondary education and English, and has written for all the top national testing companies in the United States. She lives in the Pacific Northwest with her kids and husband and spends as much time reading as she can. Being an author is the best possible job she can imagine. She loves to travel and has already added China to her list of eventual destinations.